PRAISE FOR *1968*

"Anthony Walton's *1968* sees Dr. Martin Luther King's assassination, through the eyes of youth, music, love, and awe: a near-impossible feat, given the fraught social and familial inheritances he ponders, that he makes seem effortless. He sings of a hard-won, protected interiority ('the smallest desire for solitude, / quiet and one's own counsel'), a blues legend's loneliness ('could you be the one'), and the rapturous and blissful refuge of intimacy with a scholar's precision, historian's eye, and poet's soul, carefully stitching the late 20th century's trauma inside our bodies and minds, to a lyrical, autobiographical 'I.' No stranger to grief and catastrophe ('there is always something left / to lose'), and tragic irony ('Alzheimer's' portrays an ailing father beset by memory loss, whose disease's name darkly echoes possession by another), *1968* is a masterstroke of a collection that solidifies Walton's stature as the poetic conscience of our times, giving beauty for sorrow, readerly tenderness for alienation, and, through these 'elaborations in darkness,' a jazz spiritual solo so anthemic, and romantic devotion so pure, it astounds: 'the blue light / painting the night.'"

—Virginia Konchan

"There is something wonderfully natural about Anthony Walton's poems. This calm (but not too casual) approach comes out of a prosaic style of winding but straightforward sentences/lines, and an address sometimes to 'you,' a particular beloved, but also the reader. The voice is not so emotional as to exclude history or a knowledge of music, particularly the blues. Throughout these poems we witness a poet who is a listener and a reader. His invention is quiet yet brings us into wise meditation alongside the writer. You have to slow down to parse phrasings such as 'true love and its fraternal twin, the blues' and 'indifference . . . condescension as self-pity' or 'to worry and work a rosary / of history and fate, to contemplate / love and hate.' Reading these poems, I'm reminded of my favorite Frank O'Hara, but here is someone even more believably intimate, or intimately believable lifting up his unique voice."

—John Poch

"It's rare for a single slim volume of poetry to offer both amplitude and ampleness: reading *1968* left me wowed by Anthony Walton's range of subjects and moods, and satisfied by a sense of completion at the book's end. His polyphonic recital of national tragedy and personal reckonings drew me, gratefully, 'into the everloving arms of the mortal world.'"

   —Megan Marshall

"In *1968*, Anthony Walton skillfully weaves love poems with meditations on civil rights, music, and American history, creating a lyric archive of a nation fractured by assassinations and cultural upheaval while giving voice to iconic artists—Gwendolyn Brooks, Etta James, Irma Thomas, Smokey and Aretha—figures who embody our collective inheritance. Throughout this book, Walton offers us the straight story, not only 'low-toned rumors of the wind.' Steeped in the cadence of rhythm and blues, this unforgettable collection offers a testament to survival, desire, and the enduring work of lived memory."

   —Eileen Cleary

1968

1968

Anthony Walton

Staircase Books
Cambridge, Massachusetts

First edition

editors@staircasebooks.org
staircasebooks.org

ISBN: 978-1-960769-07-7

CONTENTS

For Heather

1968

Five years since I sat in my father's sad
tensed lap while the black and white

rites for the President cast a shadow
through a vast and sinister November
night
          through our tiny flickering Philco

(the widow's black gloves, dress, and netted
veil shot straight through with static).

Five years after that I devoted myself to drinking
so much bottled Fanta and cans of Nehi

that my tongue bloomed the orange-pink
of the hide of a Sendak carnivore,

that woodland creature who threatened to devour
the child whole.
                    So I became a scout, and mastered the privacy

of the lurking dark until the night of the lacerating spring
killing of King. And that summer I spent my nights
in secret,

inhaling Smokey and Aretha, that helpless poetry, praying
love or sex would be the balm that kept me afloat

while I swam and survived days full of words— *Tet, Bobby, Grant
Park*—that I did not comprehend yet heard
                                        without end.

Then, that sunlit autumn there was a child
down by the Fox, skipping river rocks, singing
one love song or another, wondering

where all that water would be in a week, tomorrow,
or fifty years—

        This was before you were born, and that
boy was me, rendering with a boyish falsetto
his dirge for a world that he knew
was already beyond him—

saying a little prayer,
and waiting for you—

THE ENCYCLOPEDIA OF RHYTHM AND BLUES

Passion killings plane crashes overdoses
accidental and intended

Suicides bus wrecks women the inability to choose
between one woman and another

heroin booze the inability to choose
between pleasure

and the Lord men prison the white man
the white man who owns

the record company the melismatic celebration
of disaster the gut-wrenching agony

of joy the anger and hush of the naked soul alone
sighing and shouting intensely hyperbolic

declarations of erotic heroism—*anywhere, baby,
anyhow*—skidding out of control and into the next-

to-the-last chorus and over the bridge and key
change, popping the balloon of a heart inflated

with humiliation and pain and replacing it
with guttural and shrieking glissandos

—*I once was lost and now am found*—
as if a singer were an angel commissioned

in the highest holy orders, as if a song had wings
extended into flight and feathers of shelter—

as if true love and its fraternal twin, the blues,
possessed equally the powers of devotion

and redemption, as if the one true heaven
were standing around the corner, laughing

drunk, and locked with lust and abandon
into the everloving arms of the mortal world.

HOMAGE TO IRMA THOMAS

Rain taps on roof and window, making me remember
you, making me forget water is clear, not blue.

ETTA JAMES CONTEMPLATES PENELOPE AS SHE SURVEYS THE ITHACA OF ANOTHER SUNDAY MORNING

Waiting
for a man, waiting

for the world
to turn,

for Tyree, the
recalcitrant pianist,

to get back
from getting high.

She pulls, puffs and stubs
another butt.

So tired, she hauls herself
to the mic

and with deeply styled sighs
pleads and proclaims her

plight—too many Saturday
nights, her whiskey

voice an unfiltered slow drag
of the blues:

baby, baby, baby
could you be the one?

Tired dreams, blistered love
and tribulation—

then waking to the yawning
empty bed of another

Sunday morning:
nothing

but two aspirin,
baby, straighten

the covers, brush
your teeth—

GWENDOLYN BROOKS

(1917–2000)

Sometimes I see in my mind's eye a four- or five-
year-old boy, coatless and wandering
a windblown and vacant lot or street in Chicago
on the windblown South Side. He disappears
but stays with me, staring and pronouncing
me guilty of an indifference more callous
than neglect, condescension as self-pity.

Then I see him again, at ten or fifteen, on the corner,
say, 47th and Martin Luther King, or in a group
of men surrounding a burning barrel off Lawndale,
everything surrounding condemned or for sale.
Sometimes I trace him on the train to Joliet
or Menard, such towns quickly becoming native
ground to these boys who seem to be nobody's
sons, these boys who are so hard to love, so hard
to see, except as case studies.

Poverty, pain, shame, one and a half million
dreams deemed fit only for the most internal
of exiles. That four-year-old wandering
the wind tunnels of Robert Taylor, of Cabrini
Green, wind chill of an as yet unplumbed degree—
a young boy she did not have to know to love.

DRIVE-BY

It was one of those furious
seasons on the South Side
when even a gentle and quiet child
was not allowed to sit on his porch
and contemplate the sky. It was
one of those summers when the wars
between various factions of the gangs,
various factions of the police, and
various manifestations of sociology,
biology and real estate conspired
to assassinate him as he sat mildly
contemplating, in my mind, passages
from Langston Hughes, Richard
Wright, and Isaac Asimov. He was
so private, bookish and *private*,
in a city and circumstance where
the smallest desire for solitude,
quiet and one's own counsel
is construed a threat to the public
and privatized powers-that-be.

*

If it is a truism to say black men
are built out of the church or the street,
then this innocent made himself in
the library, his appetite, no, *need*
for books legend among teachers,
family, friends, a hunger that gained
sympathy even among those who
could not comprehend such urgency,
his humorous and black-rimmed, near-
sighted run for knowledge, while his
soon-to-be executioners ran guns and

stolen cars through kaleidoscopes
of heat and rage on the way to prison,
to an uncounted number of fair and unfair
early deaths, daring anyone in sight
to defy. But the imperatives
of territory and adolescence were
nothing to him until some fool
decided that any sixteen-year-old
with a certain skin tone and that zip
code had to ride or die, choose a side.

Pick a side, pick a side, pick a side—

The ferocious, hungry, and guileless
imagination provided no place to hide.
If an innocent would not murder,
his alternative was to die.

But that was a long time ago.
There was, one might say, another
Black boy left behind, left in the stacks
to worry and work a rosary
of history and fate, to contemplate
love and hate, counting the beads
of those who did and did not escape—

Cousin, scholar, statistic—
who would I not kill
to bring you home?

SØREN KIERKEGAARD WRITES TO REGINE OLSEN ON THE DAY OF HER MARRIAGE TO FRITZ SCHLEGEL

I have been reading again the story of Abraham
and Isaac,
contemplating our task, the way
we must be ever at the ready
to surrender
whatever it is Our Lord
would have us surrender.

You are my sacrifice, the unconsummated wife
of my soul, and I was all too eager
to prove how much I loved you,
loved *Him*, by being willing
to give you up. Like Abraham, like
Isaac, I was led by my beliefs to believe
we would both be spared.
I was protecting you
from the evil of this age, the evil
in myself. I wanted Him
to bless our union,
and I wanted to wear that blessing like a shield.

I cannot rescind my leap of faith.
I have sent a small gift, but will not
attend the wedding. If, after the service,
you should chance to look
toward the hill above Deer Park,
you may consider yourself free
to imagine that you see me,
standing in the full realization
that I have misunderstood the deity.

The world, Regine, is a killing
machine, each thing searching
for some smaller thing, greased
and driven by a grist wheel
of cruelty. We spend our lives walking,
swimming through the fetid
bloody swamps of our deeds.
I did not mean to choose Him
over you. Can you forgive me
my faith? Can you see that I let you go
only that you should return?
Darling, I would not have harmed you.

ARKHÊ KAKÔN

The Greeks knew things happen:

to the man working on his tractor
who lifts his head to find

his brother-in-law standing there,
hands clasped, speechless—

to the woman who wakes from dreamless
sleep in a fluorescent room without

windows to find she is no longer
considered legally sane—

to the disaster-wracked, freshly homeless
voices on the radio, the grainy

litany of their lives, a song
of 'never the same'—

*

We recognize the symbols:

in the sirens' pierce, the blue light
painting the night, flags folded

into tight isosceles, flowers
strewn on newly pregnant graves,

rosaries stroked in lieu
of the beloved's hand—

at the ocean's ebb or edge, a man
on television stares past the camera

and says, "sometimes you ain't lucky
enough to get killed."

*

So we invoke the patience of Job,

who argued with the sky—
and Akhmatova and her woman without a face

who knew that there is always something left
to lose, a grief beyond description—

except for the lean of a lone tree along
a ridge, or the silent, roof-torn

torched car along the road, or the man
in a black suit, inching from a taxi—

the moment when pain becomes
memory: one remembers to remember

those they cannot forget, to let
them go wherever

it is they must go, and wait.

ALZHEIMER'S

He sits, silent,
no longer mistaking the cable
news for company—

and when he speaks, he speaks of childhood,
remembering some slight or conundrum
as if it is a score to be retailed

and settled after seventy-five years.

Rare, the sudden lucidity
that acknowledges *this thing*
that has happened
to me ...

More often, he recounts
his father's cruelty
or a chance deprived
to him, a Negro
            under Jim Crow.

Five minutes ago escapes him
as he chases 1934, unaware

of the present beauty out the window,
the banks of windswept snow—

or his wife, humming in the kitchen,
or the twilit battles in Korea, or me

when he remembers I am his son.

This condition—with a name that implies
the proprietary,
possession,
                    spiritual
and otherwise—

as if it owns him,
which it does.

AGAINST FACEBOOK

I have no desire to reconnect
with Bobby from wood shop, wanting
to sell me insurance

or sparkplugs—

nor Sheldon, strangely full of latter-day
remorse for stealing *Kind of Blue*
and *Hotel California* from my dorm
room at Colby—

I do not wish to be found by Wendy, yearning
to recapture (what I admit I may have felt
as well) a moment of electricity

between us at the company picnic

that year when we both were assigned
to Carol Stream.

I prefer to be alone, dreaming of a software
much grander and infinitely more useful—

a platform that would not link, but
launch   a catapult to propel me from cyberspace

into space-time:

an American flight from Dallas to Salt Lake,
August 2008, and the elaborately-coiffed
attendant who noticed me reading *Praise*
and who with her arm

across the seatback leaned into me
and recited from memory
the poem on page 27.

I need an algorithm that will calculate
and create the astronomic telemetry
from here to Francine Jackson,

the high school beauty I loved
as a freshman, so far and so strangely
above me she may as well have been
a constellation. Zuckerberg, build something

useful, something

that gives me back that evening on Lighthouse
Beach the year I lived in Evanston, Aphrodite
herself stroking the thick ruff of her retriever
as she looked

up and smiled with so much heat and kindness
that I kept walking, stunned, thinking
then and most days since,

what if—

PERSONAL

I am who I am
younger than you
might think though
older than I
thought possible
Like everybody
I like sunsets
hiking, baseball
and movies; also
were the Lord
in His wisdom
to bless me
with a sailboat
I am sure I would
enjoy sailing. I like
to see myself in my
mind lying on a
sailboat gazing
at the stars I like
to see myself
as adventurous
a rebel and a dreamer
someone willing
to take chances
I am nice looking
and intelligent, honest
shy, caring, sensitive
and open-minded
Nothing to write home
about, though
you would not
be embarrassed
or ashamed
to take me home

to your mother
or your apartment
I am not opposed
to children, yours
or ours I am
who I am
which is to say
because you are
reading this
you

BEFORE THE STORM

Another night of wanting you
here—
        so much to tell

you, elaborations in darkness

tracing the fault lines
                 of a man driving

at 3 AM, listening for certainty in the leaves
as they rustle with conspiracies

and low-toned rumors of the wind—

were you here, you might witness
the great horned owl frozen and backlit

by lightning as it blew across our path,
                         wings flared

and justified

as if the frame of the windshield
were a blazing blue-tinted

photograph—
                I would not be left to contemplate

the paranoia of trees, or to dredge the welter
of my disarray—

we could talk, as meticulous as these first few
moments of rain.

MARRIAGE

In bed, naked and after,
reading, silently, annotated
copies of the same book.

DEAD RECKONING

We are driving the Middle West, lost
as Oklahoma or Kansas slowly
spins into darkness.

Hard red winter wheat
leans with the wind while the knife of 83
bisects sunlight barely over
the near horizon.

I try not to remember what has happened
here, bloody grass prairie, Comanche
and Kiowa Wars—

wondering why I can't forget
and simply love that she is here with me, unfolding
a map to determine where we are
and how long it is
until Salina or Amarillo, Wichita

Falls or Muskogee. With painted nail
she idly traces a crossroads
and I imagine her conjuring a younger self
on a screened porch

on a gravel county road, conducting love songs
from the radio, but before I finish
composing my fantasy she frowns
and notes that we are traversing

the Greater Seminole Field, and I am startled
to notice the oil pumps and derricks—
the population of iron scarecrows
and skeletons—

she lightly takes my hand, holding
me inside the car, this
thin shell of transit

and safety, as if to say
be still—be still and remember
last night, and the night
to come—

NOTES

HOMAGE TO IRMA THOMAS

Ms. Thomas (b. 1941, Ponchatoula, Louisiana) is a legendary New Orleans rhythm and blues artist. In terms of this poem, cf. "It's Raining," Minit Records, written and produced by Allen Toussaint.

ETTA JAMES CONTEMPLATES PENELOPE AS SHE SURVEYS THE ITHACA OF ANOTHER SUNDAY MORNING

Ms. James (1938–2012), another legend of rhythm and blues, known for her ability to turn any sort of popular song, including standards such as "A Sunday Kind of Love" and "At Last," into unique and personal expressions of longing, tinged with despair.

GWENDOLYN BROOKS

Although she was born in Topeka, Kansas, Ms. Brooks (1917–2000), spent most of her life in Chicago, where she was particularly devoted to African American youth. She was the first Black person to receive a Pulitzer Prize, in 1950, and served as Poet Laureate of the United States, and of the state of Illinois.

SØREN KIERKEGAARD WRITES TO REGINE OLSEN ON THE DAY OF HER MARRIAGE TO FRITZ SCHLEGEL

Existential philosopher Kierkegaard broke his engagement to Regine Olsen in 1841. He was said to have experienced deep regret for doing so the rest of his life. This poem is, as a dramatic monologue, an imagined recreation of Regine's wedding day, as Kierkegaard observed the festivities from a hill above Copenhagen.

ARKHÊ KAKÔN

One translation of the title of this poem (from the Greek) is "the beginning of bad things," which I learned from Daniel Mendelsohn's *An Odyssey: A Father, A Son, and an Epic* (Alfred A. Knopf, 2017).

ACKNOWLEDGMENTS

I would like to express my gratitude to the editors of the following journals in which versions of these poems first appeared: Honore Fanonne Jeffers, Langdon Hammer, Quincy Troupe, David Lynn, Alice Quinn, Kevin Young, Danny Lawless, and John Poch.

Academy of American Poets' "Poem-a-Day": "Alzheimer's"

The American Scholar: "1968," "Arkhê Kakôn," "Against Facebook," "Marriage"

Black Renaissance Noire: "Homage to Irma Thomas," "Drive-by"

Kenyon Review: "Søren Kierkegaard Writes to Regine Olsen on the Day of Her Marriage to Fritz Schlegel"

The New Yorker: "The Encyclopedia of Rhythm and Blues," "Gwendolyn Brooks," and "Dead Reckoning"

Plume: "Before the Storm"

32 Poems: "Personal" (reprinted in *Verse Daily* as "Poem-of-the-Day")

An early version of "Etta James Contemplates Penelope as She Surveys the Ithaca of Another Sunday Morning" appeared in a limited-edition chapbook, *Cricket Weather* (Blackberry Books, 1995).

I would like to thank George Makari, Claudette Walton, Richard Ford, Gary Lawless and Beth Leonard, the late Michael S. Harper, and James Fraser and Bella Bennett. I would also like to thank Valerie Upham, Deborah Murphy, and the English Department and administration at Bowdoin College. Finally, a thank you to the ubiquitous Maren, and to Heather Treseler, without whom.

Anthony Walton's poems have appeared widely, in such magazines and journals as *The New Yorker, The American Scholar, The Black Scholar, 32 Poems, Alaska Quarterly Review, Kenyon Review, Black Renaissance Noire, Poetry Ireland, Oxford American, Obsidian, Notre Dame Review, The Library of America,* and *The Academy of American Poets.* A celebrated writer of prose, he is the author of *Mississippi: An American Journey* and *The End of Respectability,* among other books. With the late Michael S. Harper, he edited two landmark anthologies, *Every Shut-eye Ain't Asleep: African American Poetry Since World War II,* and *The Vintage Anthology of African American Poetry.*

The typefaces used for *1968* are Portrait and
GRAPHIK EXTENDED by Commercial Type.

The book was printed by Bookmobile in an edition
of 400 copies.